# HOW TO CONVERT MORE VISITORS

## TO CUSTOMERS USING A PAGELESS WEBSITE

Gus Skarlis Founder MobileWebsites.com

# Contents

# *Pageless Design*

Many of the most innovative companies have transitioned over to pageless design as a method of redefining the way that users experience the web. Pageless design has many advantages over traditional design and is expected to rapidly become a popular new web standard. A unique format that works by enhancing the advantages of web media rather than trying to reproduce a print media layout, some view pageless design as a natural evolution of web design.

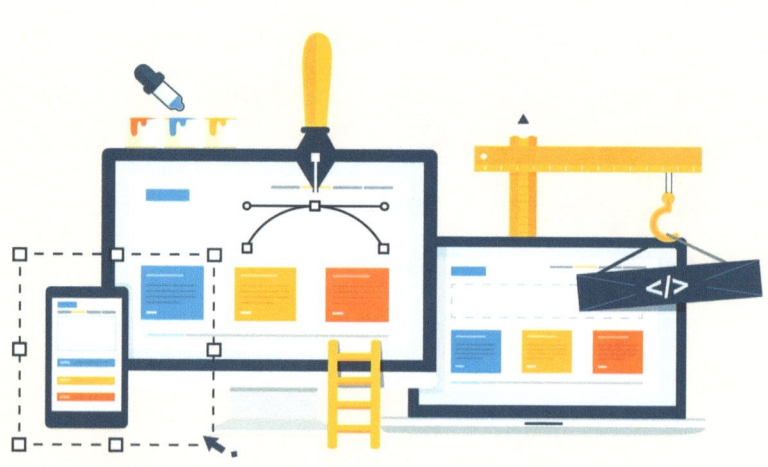

DESIGN DEVELOPMENT

# *Market Drivers: User Engagement Supports a Pageless Design*

User engagement is the primary driving force behind most website developments today, especially as the focus has switched from raw traffic to conversion rates. The web audience has a tendency to have a short attention span, resist clicking on too many links and avoid content that will take too long to scroll through. Users who are more engaged will be far more likely to convert on a website, making increasing participation one of the major goals for any company.

The primary challenges to user engagement are usually as follows:

- Technical issues with the website itself.
- Disinterest from the user, often due to subverted expectations.

Technical glitches with the website don't necessarily mean that the website itself is broken. Something as simple as a delay of a few seconds could cause a user to leave the website. Traditionally, this challenge has been countered by optimizing websites so that they load quickly and ensuring that websites are easily viewed on every possible platform.

A lack of user interest is a more complex problem. A lack of engagement once the user has already arrived at the page is often cause by them not finding what they were looking for on the website itself. This often occurs if the user is driven to arrive at the website with an expectation that the website itself does not meet. Clever search engine optimization and precise social media and advertising techniques are used to ensure that the user's expectations are met.

Though there are conventional techniques that increase user engagement, pageless design is a method of website design that directly counters many of these challenges automatically, without the need for other strategies and tactics.

Pageless designs encourage user engagement by drawing users into the site immediately.

A pageless design will load its above the fold content very quickly, thereby reducing the possibility that the user may become frustrated at long wait times and click away from the page.

Rather than forcing the user to select a location of the site and click through to it, a pageless design offers the user an interactive and simple experience that offers the freedom to follow but not the confusion of choice.

The simple act of scrolling down engages the user in a form of storytelling and the continued content will keep them on the site for longer than clicking through a multitude of similar pages would. Often, a user will scroll down automatically as content is revealed to them; the same automatic response does not generally happen with clicking links.

By its very nature, a pageless design is an extremely interactive format. As the user scrolls downwards, the page will continue to produce more content. Though subtle, this act of revealing content to the user as they demand it will give the user a sense of control over the website and heighten their sense of interactivity and engagement. Stimulating a user's engagement is always a good idea because it increases their investment in the website and leads to them wanting to learn more.

Pageless design essentially tells a story to the user. It's offers a web experience rather than a simple set of web pages. While scrolling through the design, the user gradually learns more in a chronological sequence; it also gives the website developers complete control over the order of the user experience and thus makes it far easier to keep the experience consistent and coherent.

Ultimately, a pageless design creates a seamless user experience which is not interrupted or distracted from, thereby increasing both user engagement and conversion rates. This ensures that the website has the best possible chance of keeping the user engaged throughout a session and that the user will not become distracted or move away from the site at any time. This benefits the ultimate need to increase user engagement and the potential for user conversions.

# Where Pageless Design Excels Over Conventional Design

Many users will leave websites for the following reasons: they become disinterested, the content doesn't load fast enough or they can't find the information they need on the first page. Most bounce rights can be attributed to one of these three issues, and pageless websites are able to fix all of these issues with a simple, clean and concise format change. Conventional designs may obscure or hide information and make

the user hunt for it; this is something that can quickly turn into frustration.

Pageless websites are ultimately designed to give the user the information they desire and are geared towards concise information. All the user needs to do is scroll down to get absolutely everything they need from the website. Pageless websites sidestep issues of having to click through to get more information or having to wait for long loading periods; instead, the information is all right there and accessible. The user isn't always aware of whether the information they need is on the page, so they will be inclined to scroll down to find out more. A pageless website thus engages the consumer right away, removing user disinterest.

Conventional websites demand far more of the user. They demand that the user find the information they are interested in rather than being presented the information and then, once the information has been found, it is delivered in a large chunk. With pageless design, the user is given a compelling experience that is trickled out to them in a specific order. Through conventional design, the user is given a completely passive information experience that they have to look for.

Though loading periods cannot be completely removed through a pageless design, they can usually be hidden; while the user is reading one portion of the site, background loading occurs to ensure they will have the content they need when they scroll downwards. This removes one of the largest problems of web design: loading times. Studies have long shown that users will only wait two or three seconds for a page to load before losing interest and leaving. A pageless design resolves this incredibly major issue.

Conventional websites simply optimize their media as much as possible. They may compress graphics and video, but this isn't always the best solution; media-heavy content is becoming very popular and some popular elements such as HD video, can only be compressed down so much. Clever loading tactics are the best way to display items like HD video rather than simply compressing them or forcing the user to wait through a loading screen.

From a structural standpoint, pageless websites are an excellent way to create concise and easy to read content. The format is truly designed for brevity, and this promotes a design in which the users can easily find everything they need on the same page. Designers have the freedom to avoid worrying about their above the fold or below the fold content--to some extent--and can instead focus on creating a solid and seamless user experience.

Conventional websites need to concern themselves with a layout that closely mimics a print layout. They design their pages like physical pages, and this strips away much of the potential innovation that the format allows while adding another level of unnecessary complexity.

Pageless designs also allow companies to control the flow of their content. A pageless design allows the company to create a narrative and involve the user within this narrative. With a paged design, the company has no idea what content the user will see or where they will see it. Pageless designs show the content in a specific order designed to create a complete story experience.

Conventional websites may use a significant amount of links throughout their website and a structured navigation system in an attempt to ensure that users visit all of the relevant sections of their website, but they have no true control over what order the user views their website in.

# *Historical Overview of Pageless Designs*

Pageless design is not new. It has been used by market leaders for years, but it has only really come in to vogue for other sites since 2013. Most of the issues that have been holding pageless design back arose from a lack of technology and bandwidth: the ability to dynamically load a page from the bottom simply wasn't around.

However, there was another issue holding pageless design back from the start: a lack of innovaton.

From the very beginning of the web, most people saw the web as a series of connected web "pages." The web was considered like a book: you flipped from page to page. Consider the terminologies web "site," web "log," and web "page." Everything on the web was considered to be analogous to a physical item in the real world.

Pages were considered to be short items--no longer than an actual page--and sites were sectioned out into chapters. It is natural that everything was done this way: in the early days, bandwidth was so extremely limited that only a small amount of data could be transmitted at any time.

Websites had to have very brief index pages and then very brief content pages to ensure that users could load the content within a reasonable amount of time. Putting too much information on a single page would bog the user down and discourage the, from continuing.

Of course, the web is quite different from anything that had preceded it and very different from a book. It took a very long time--and a significant amount of experimentation--before web designers began to break away from this book and page model.

It took even more time for clients to understand the incredible benefits of pageless design and it took more time still for the average consumer to have an Internet connection that was fast enough to take advantage of multimedia pageless design, which could integrate infographics and videos.

Some forms of pageless design have always been popular with the artist sector; there have been many portfolios created with this method. Artists seek to engage and have a unique understanding regarding user engagement; something that many web designers have learned from.

Pageless web design was further propelled into popularity with the advent of designing for mobile devices. The easy scrolling system of a pageless design naturally lends itself to the mobile platform and is extremely easy to make responsive. With more and more consumers using mobile platforms as their preferred platform of choice, it becomes absolutely essential to develop designs that can be easily translated into the mobile platform.

The final push towards pageless design actually came from marketing. Over time, marketing targets shifted away from a need for raw traffic (hits) and towards increased conversion rates. Having a lot of pages on a website increases hits but actually lowers conversion; it increases the amount of pages viewed but lowers the chance that the user will actually buy something or contact the company.

Websites that focused on raw traffic as a metric for success became obsessed with having the viewer click on as many links on their website as possible, even if the user was never actually contacting the website or purchasing a product. This pushed many away from pageless, concentrate designs and towards larger, sprawling design patterns.

Many web design companies and marketing agencies were focusing on the wrong statistics all along. They were blindly trying to increase traffic and hits when it was really mostly conversion that mattered--and a pursuit of raw traffic was leading them in a direction that was actually detrimental to the company. Partially, this was because it's always been easier to build raw traffic than conversion rates.

A renewed focus on conversion rates in favor of raw traffic has made it so that many companies are focusing more on the user experience rather than the amount of page views that their website gets, and this is beneficial to both the companies and the users.

# Conventional Design and Other Alternatives to Pageless Design

Before pageless design, websites were either created in one of two formats: a long sequence of pages linked together or a single page that contained all of the data. Both of these formats had some clear issues that have been resolved through pageless design; pageless design can operate as a medium between the two extremes.

Traditional websites rely upon the user to click through the website, to remain engaged and to find the information they are looking for. A significant amount of time is always invested during the developmental stages to ensure that the website itself is engaging enough to keep users on the website and to prompt them to click on the links when they should. Web developers also spend a substantial amount of time trying to control and track which links users are actually clicking on.

Companies have no ultimate control over what the user sees or when. The user can click through the website in any order that they want, thus leaving the company completely in the dark about what the user "knows" when they see any given page. Some websites now track users and what they have already visited on the website to tailor the viewing experience for them.

The user experience is also fragmented in this way; users only get pieces of information rather than a whole story. They may become frustrated throughout this experience or unable to piece together the knowledge into a coherent narrative.

Every time a company asks a user to click through to another page, they run the risk that the user will simply become disinterested or frustrated and leave the site. This leads companies to worry about their bounce rates and conversion rates.

Of course, there's also another solution--one which was used during the very beginning of the web. Companies can also control the flow of their website by putting something all in one page, through a slideshow, a video or an interactive application.

In fact, before pageless design was developed and became popular, many companies would create a flash site that was on only a single page. Though this did create a holistic user experience in much the same way that a pageless design did, it came with its own problems.

This type of design, involving slideshows or videos, is by necessity very costly to produce and it is difficult to maintain and change. These websites were very expensive to make and tended to remain static for long periods of time because they were so expensive to change.

Even worse, they tended not to be shared because the content in them couldn't usually be directly linked to. Often, the users could still access information out of sequence by flipping through the slides out of order and the users would still end up lost. Flash sites did not last long--they fell out of favor with both users and developers quite quickly--but they did show that there was a desire to control the user experience more tightly than most websites would allow.

The largest issue with this type of single page web design was the loading times and the

responsiveness. These websites often took a significant amount of time to simply load; there would actually be a loading screen and a loading wheel visible for a period of time, prompting many users to leave and bounce rates to skyrocket.

Today's modern world simply won't accept this type of design because it is generally not responsive. Companies who rely, in a large part, upon slideshows and videos should keep this in mind: these tactics, though they may look good on a computer, will often not translate at all into a mobile device.

# *The Core Benefits to a Pageless Design*

There are many clear and fantastic benefits to pageless design. It allows the company to control the narrative flow of the information, it's easy for the user to move through and understand, it engages users, it increases conversion rates, it's easy to move into a responsive design, it's easy to modify, it decreases bounce rates,it encourages sharing and its even a rather inexpensive type of design.

Through a pageless design, a company is able to control exactly what information the user sees and when. Rather than simply allowing the user to freely click and scroll through data, the company knows exactly what information the user sees and the order they see it in. This allows the company to create a narrative or story around their product or service. In later sections of the website, the company will know that the user has a specific amount of knowledge and they can build on this knowledge. In a traditional paged website, the company cannot build on knowledge because the company will not be certain that the knowledge is there.

Pageless designs are user-friendly. All a user needs to do is scroll steadily downwards and everything they need will be revealed to them. The user will be able to understand the information being presented to them because it is being presented in a concise, direct way with a mix of media. The ability of the company to control narrative flow benefits the user: the user simply needs to listen to the story and they will gain all of the information they need.

Ultimately, this increases user engagement. The easier it is for the user to obtain and digest the information, the more likely it will be that the user will stay on the site and continue interacting with the site.

Engaged users are far more likely to convert. A pageless design invests the user into the website because they have shared an experience with the website and spent time on the website. Thus, the user is then more willing to convert--and conversion rates are the most important part of the web design experience.

Users who encounter a pageless design are far less likely to bounce from the website because they know the information they want is somewhere on the website. Furthermore, they are more likely to share the design because they know that the website represents a valuable experience that others might enjoy.

Pageless web designs also have a multitude of development benefits. A pageless web design is very easy to move into any responsive device; in fact, responsive devices naturally use pageless designs. Pageless web designs are also exceptionally easy to modify and maintain, leading to lower web design bills overall. A pageless web design is actually less expensive than a traditional web design because there are fewer moving parts.

# *Examples of Pageless Design*

**Uber.com**

The new taxi service Uber boasts an extremely flashy, metropolitan design that likely appeals to its core demographic. Users scroll through the homepage to find out everything they need to know about the service. Like many pageless designs, it begins with bold imagery: a large slideshow that extends across the entire screen. Scrolling down on Uber, you can easily see that the design is chunky and easy to read. The design controls when the user gets information and how they get it by letting them scroll down.

Unlike conventional designs, the menu here is not emphasized. In fact, the menu is almost hidden--it is located in the upper right corner as small text, almost as a side thought. The menu can be this small and barely emphasized because all the pertinent information on the website is on the main page.

**Lunita.ca**

An excellent example of how a restaurant can use a pageless design, the design of Lunita offers absolutely everything that a potential guest could need. The design begins with a bold picture of one of the restaurant's main dishes and urges the viewer to scroll downwards. As the user scrolls further down, they get a complete idea of what the restaurant is about. The restaurant users bold, fun colors to further craft an experience.

Users are initially greeted with some information about the current events at Lunita, followed by reservations, menus and contact options. These are the three major options that anyone visiting a restaurant's website would need and they are shown right away, thus giving the user the ability to quickly find the information they need. The exceptionally attractive website users dynamic pop-ups within the page rather than separate pages to ensure that the user remains engaged on the website. Lunita doesn't require raw traffic at all, being a restaurant, and thus is free to remain focused on engagement.

**Seora.co**
Seora.co shows that a pageless design does not have to be exceptionally dynamic to be powerful. The design of Seora, an Italian design company, is actually deceptively simple. The website simply offers all of the information

that a customer would require on a single page website and nothing more, nothing less. As with most pageless and mobile-friendly designs, the images are bold, high quality and expansive: pageless designs are often denoted by images that go up against the border of the window.

Also of note is the way Seora.co displays in the window initially: a single, large advertisement that takes advantage of the entire window. This would usually be frowned upon in traditional design methods but is welcomed in pageless design because of the ease at which it can be navigated through.

**Paypal.com**
Many probably don't think of Paypal when they think pageless design--especially because of how complex and involved the website is--but the homepage of Paypal is actually an excellent example of pageless design. Paypal only recently adopted its pageless design, which features high quality HD videos on their front page. Everything a user new to Paypal would need is featured on their front page now, as opposed to prior designs which required a significant amount of navigating.

When first arriving to Paypal.com, you arrive

at the pageless equivalent of a "splash" page--a front-facing graphic that captures attention. Scrolling down, you arrive at all of the details about the site itself. The website explains all of the benefits of Paypal to the user and it ends at the very bottom with a call to action: a button that reads "Mind your money."

## Quickbooks.com

Quickbooks.com is an excellent example of how pageless design can be seen as a logical extension of an advertisement. Though Quickbooks is not utilizing pageless design as much as some other companies, it still does have all of the basics of a solid pageless site. It walks the user through the experience and benefits of Quickbooks step by step, explaining to them what the product is and why it will make them easier.

As with a true pageless design, the website ends at the bottom with a call to action asking the user to set up a free trial account. Quickbooks.com is notable because it still relies upon some traditional design characteristics and it isn't as bold as many other pageless designs, but it's still an excellent example of the technology overall.

## Squareup.com

In comparison to Quickbooks.com, Squareup

actually has a much bolder pageless design. Above the fold is a brightly colored splash. The page is brief, concise and explains everything a user might need to know about Squareup as a product. The website connects to the Squareup market and, unlike Quickbooks, the call to action is the first thing the user sees rather than the last; the last section is directed towards the market, which can still be seen as a method of conversion, just a more indirect one.

Like many pageless designs, the Squareup design is chunky and friendly. It is obviously easily translated into a web design and can be managed easily and effectively by the developer.

### lutopi.com
This award-winning design website is one of the best examples of a pageless design. As you scroll through this website, the graphics move and interact with you. The design takes you step by step through lutopi's creative process and the benefits of the company and they use their design to underscore their major points. The design is exceptionally easy to navigate and entirely pageless, brightly colored and very easy to convert to a mobile device.

lutopi has a very tight, simple copy displayed

over fun and engaging images that create a user experience rather than simply a website. When viewing Iutopi, you can see the website as a sequence of advertisements. Each point they make is allowed to land: the simplicity of the website gives each point additional impact.

As with other pageless designs, Iutopi ends with a call to action: information about where and how to contact the designers. Notably, the website also ends with credits. Credits may seem strange for a website, but for a pageless website it does not: the experience of going through Iutopi is more akin to the experience of watching a short film than it is clicking through a website.

# Implementing a Website With a Pageless Design

Creating a pageless website design is usually an extremely simple process, especially when compared to the generic solutions offered by other methods of web design. Through a pageless design, you simply seek to tell a story. You can consider your story in a sequence of acts which are gradually revealed to the user. The story can be a mix of media: text, images and even videos. As the user slowly reveals more of the story, they will learn more about your services and your products. The user experience is always the essential component to increasing conversion rates.

Unlike other designs, a pageless design needs to be considered in a chronological sequence with elements of interactivity. Various forms of media are often used in pageless design, from videos to graphics. The company needs to consider its design in terms of what the user will see and when rather than simply what the user will see. At every step, the company must focus on providing a user experience that will compel the user forward.

A pageless design is, by necessity, tighter than ordinary website designs; the website should be as brief and concise as possible while remaining interesting and engaging. A significant amount of thought must be put into the copy of the website to ensure that it both remains appealing and answers any questions that the user might have.

A side effect of taking control away from the user is that you need to offer them everything they could potentially desire; otherwise you run the risk of alienating the user rather than pleasing them. You can only take control over what the user sees and the user experience overall if you are absolutely certain that you can provide the with everything they are looking for.

Otherwise, pageless design is actually quite a lot simpler than many traditional designs and should not be significantly technically complicated. Most web developers will find that pageless designs can be crafted fairly easily and, even better, can be updated quickly. The ability to maintain and update a pageless design with ease will ultimately reduce costs.

# *Getting Started in Pageless Design*

Pageless design contributes to a website in many significant ways. It creates a holistic user experience, controls the narrative of the information, promotes user engagement and conversion, reduces bounce rates, is naturally responsive, costs less to develop and is easier to maintain.

Pageless designs give web developers more control over the experience that the user has. Every user will have more or less the same experience with the website, leading to less guess work. The ability to easily modify the website and maintain it also allows for advanced testing; developers can quickly change the website to attempt to increase their conversion rates.

Not only are pageless designs better for developers, but they're also preferable for users. Users don't have to struggle to find the information they need on a website; the information they desire is simply offered up to them. Users also have a better experience through user design overall; the content given is unique, engaging and concise. They don't have to sift through endless volumes of information and pages.

Companies that will benefit the most from pageless design are companies that are tilted more towards increasing their conversion rates and providing a user experience. Companies that focus more on raw traffic or advertising revenue may find that conventional design tactics still work well for them.

It is no coincidence that many of the major players in the web development industry and many large corporations are switching to pageless design rather than keeping their conventional design methods. These companies have undergone significant volumes of market testing and research and have determined that pageless design is the way of the future.

Pageless design is the future of the web and the future of mobile-friendly design. Companies interested in moving to a pageless design should contact us at MobileWebsites.com to find out more about the process and the many incredible benefits over conventional design.

# *About MobileWebsites. com*

Since 2009, MobileWebsites.com has been creating cutting edge websites for the mobile platform. MobileWebsites.com is a full service company that offers customers not only a custom mobile website but also marketing and search engine optimization. You can even build your own website through MobileWebsites.com or request expertise from the many knowledgeable staff members.

Since being founded, the focus of MobileWebsites. com has always been to create a one stop shop for all of a company's mobile needs. The platform offers a tremendous amount of freedom in creating an unstoppable mobile website and is backed by the many years of experience of its founder, Gus Skarlis. Gus Skarlis is a technology expert and the "Go To" resource for small businesses, professionals and entrepreneurs who want to expand their mobile reach.

With offices in both Las Vegas, NV and Mason City, IA the talented staff of MobileWebsites.com is standing by to help you develop your new pageless or mobile website.

www.ingramcontent.com/pod-product-compliance
Lightning Source LLC
Chambersburg PA
CBHW052100170526
45159CB00019BA/801